AUDIO ACCESS INCLUDED
Recorded Backing Tracks Online

 T0055787

Praise AND Worship
SOLOS FOR TEENS

10 Songs with Instrumental Backing Tracks

Audio Arrangements by Larry Moore

To access companion recorded backing tracks online, visit:
www.halleonard.com/mylibrary

Enter Code
7875-6056-1781-6830

ISBN 978-1-4803-5226-1

 HAL•LEONARD®
CORPORATION
7777 W. BLUEMOUND RD. P.O.BOX 13819 MILWAUKEE, WI 53213

Visit Hal Leonard Online at
www.halleonard.com

CONTENTS

Audio Arrangements by Larry Moore

Amazing Grace
(My Chains Are Gone)

Words by JOHN NEWTON
Traditional American Melody
Additional Words and Music by CHRIS TOMLIN
and LOUIE GIGLIO

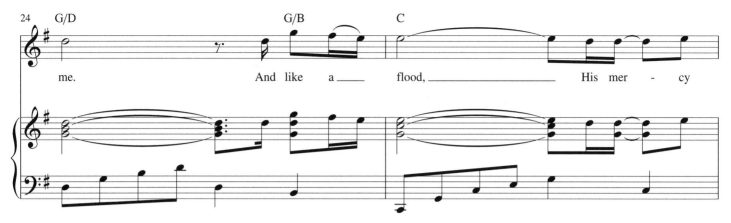

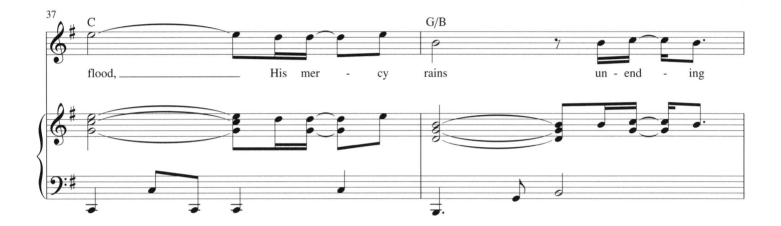

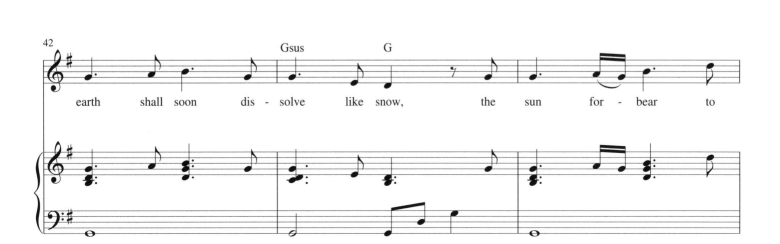

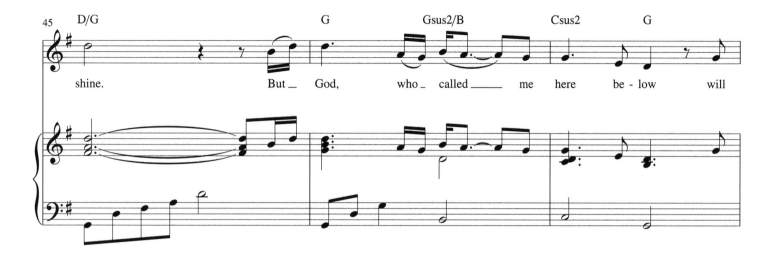

shine. But _ God, who _ called _____ me here be - low will

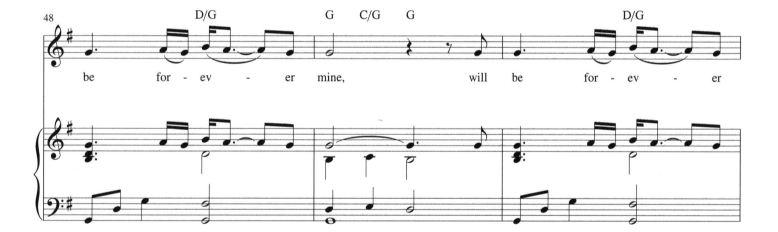

be for - ev - er mine, will be for - ev - er

mine. You are for - ev - er mine.

Hosanna

Words and Music by
BROOKE FRASER

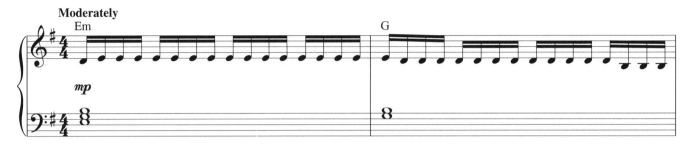

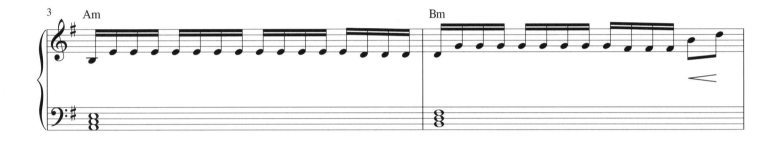

I see the King of ___ Glo — ry
I see a gen — er — a — tion

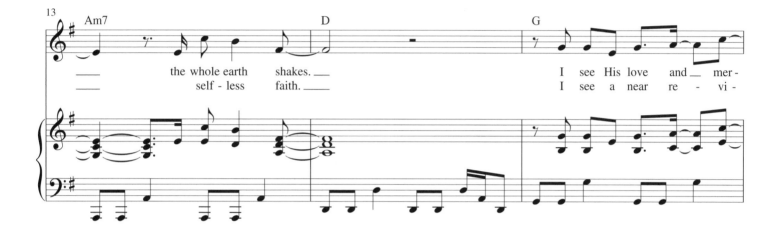

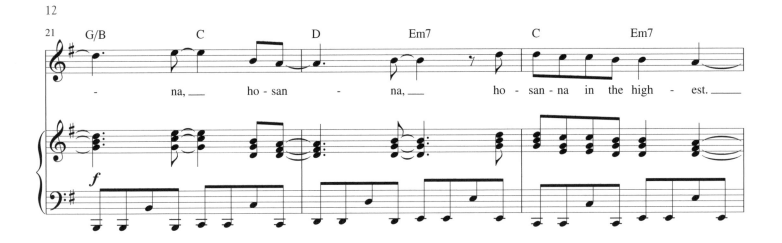

- na, ___ ho - san __ na, __ ho - san-na in the high - est. ___

___ Ho - san __ na, __ ho - san __ na, __ ho -

san - na in the high - est. ___

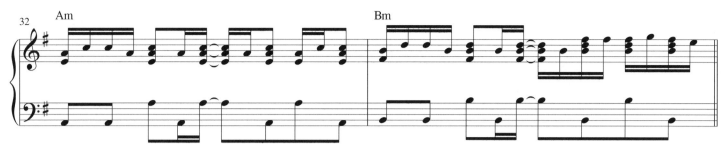

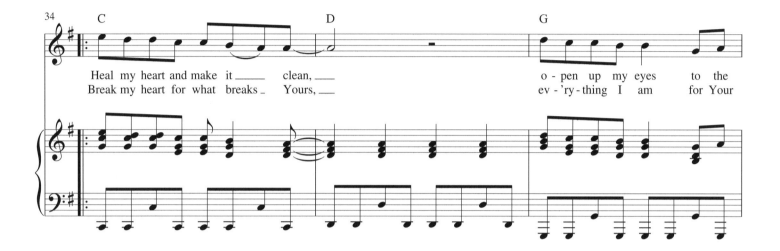

Heal my heart and make it ____ clean, ___ o - pen up my eyes to the
Break my heart for what breaks _ Yours, ___ ev - 'ry - thing I am for Your

things un - seen. _ Show me how to love like _ You ___ have loved me.
King - dom's _ cause, ___ as I walk from earth in - to ___

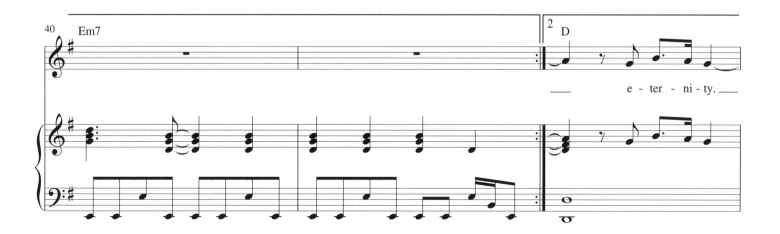

___ e - ter - ni - ty. ___

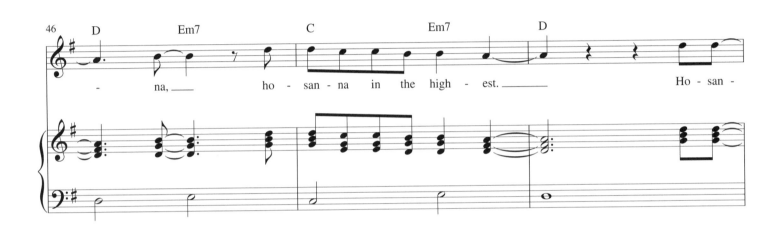

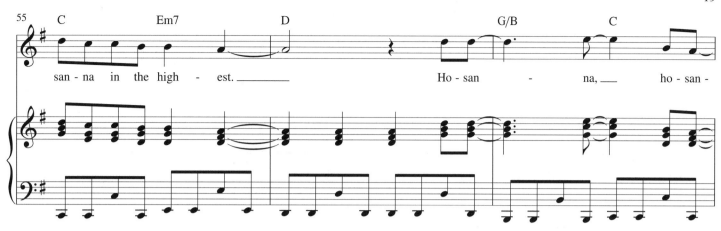

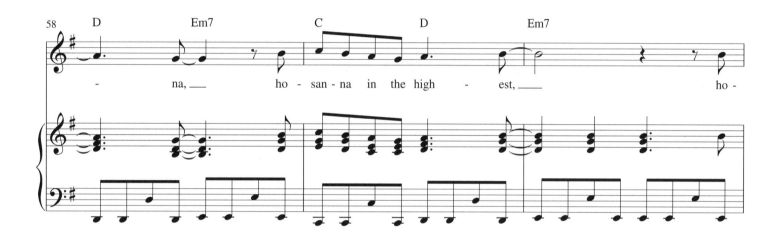

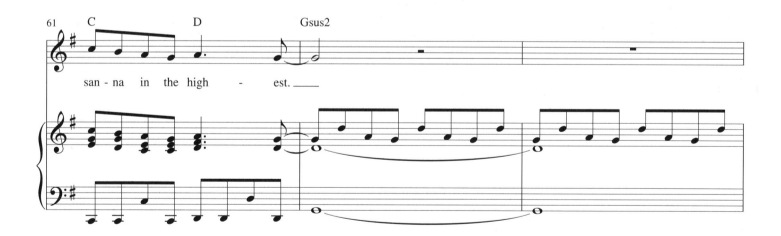

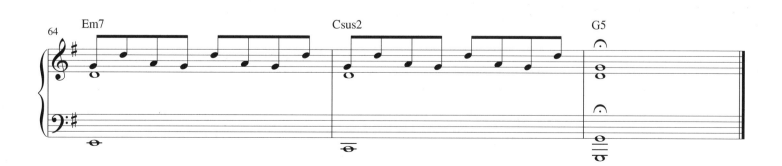

Jesus Messiah

Words and Music by CHRIS TOMLIN,
JESSE REEVES, DANIEL CARSON
and ED CASH

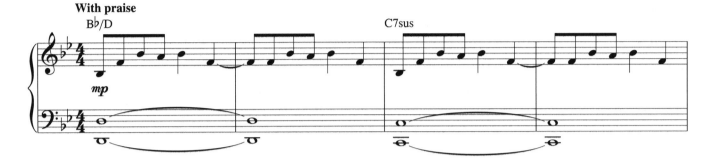

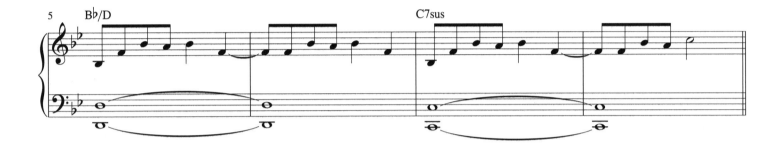

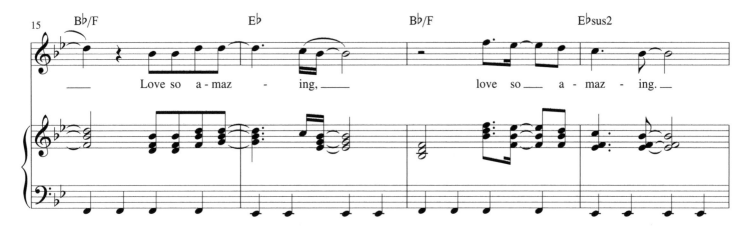

Love so a - maz - ing, love so a - maz - ing.

Je - sus Mes - si - ah, Name a - bove all

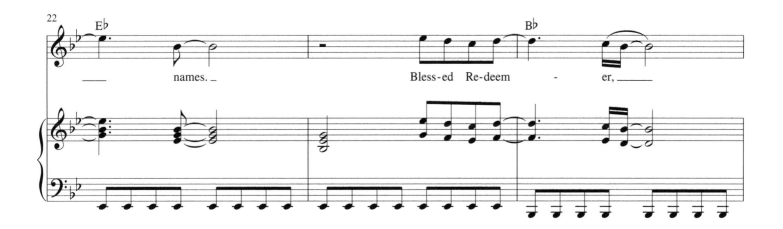

names. Bless - ed Re - deem - er,

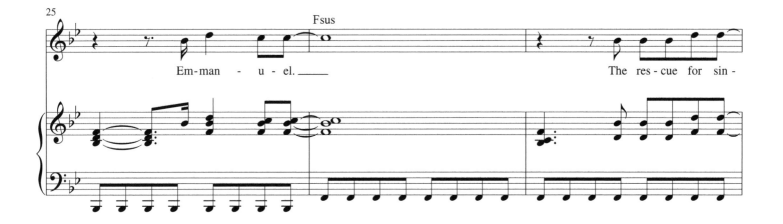

Em - man - u - el. The res - cue for sin -

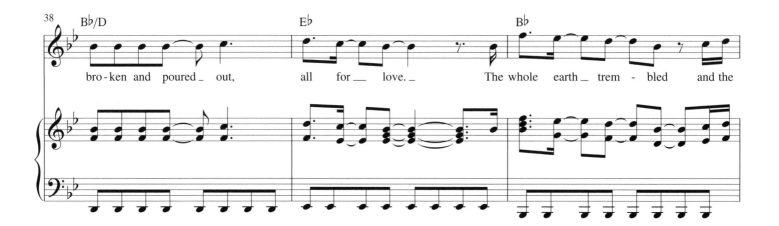

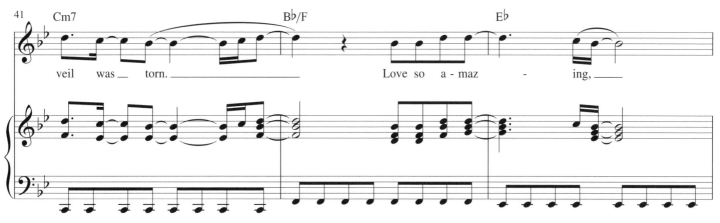

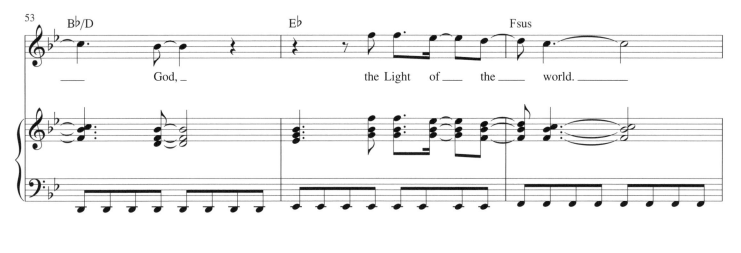

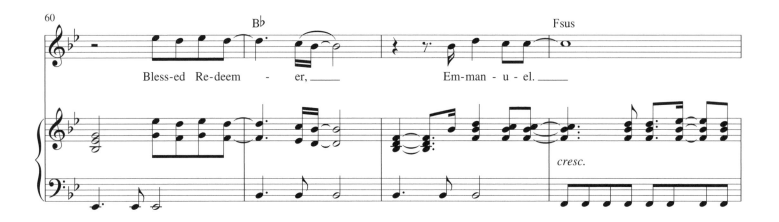

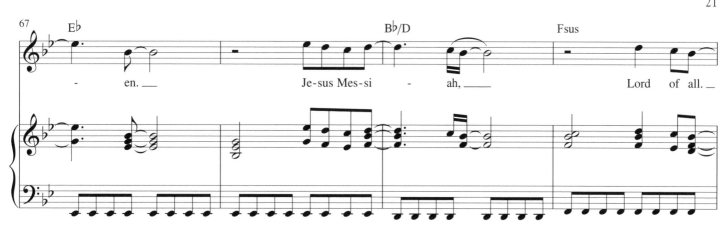

-en. ___ Je-sus Mes-si - ah, ___ Lord of all. __

___ Je-sus Mes-si - ah, ___ Lord of all. __

___ You're the Lord _ of all, ___

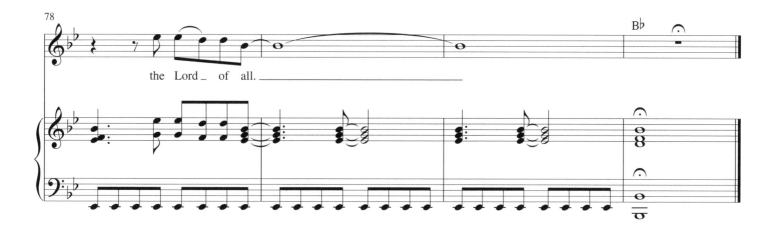

the Lord _ of all. ___

Mighty to Save

Words and Music by BEN FIELDING
and REUBEN MORGAN

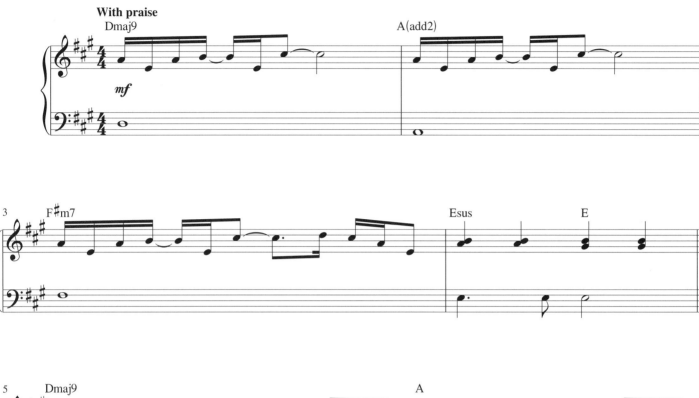

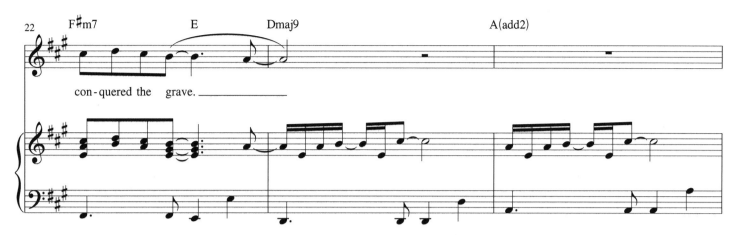

con-quered the grave._____

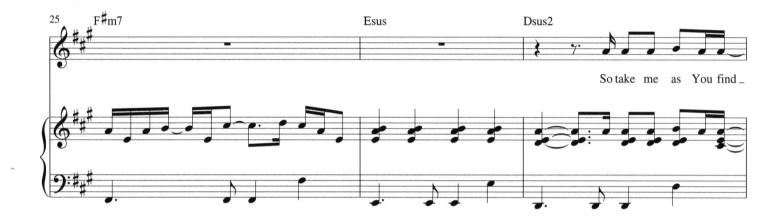

So take me as You find_

_____ me, all my fears and fail - ures; fill my life a - gain. _

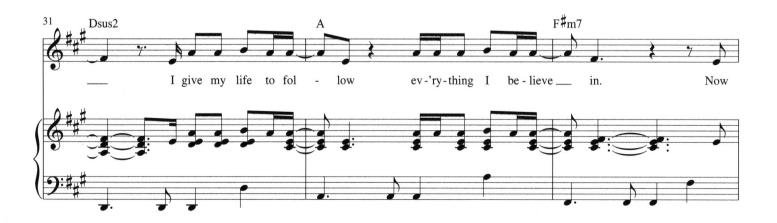

_____ I give my life to fol - low ev-'ry-thing I be-lieve_ in. Now

D.S. al Coda

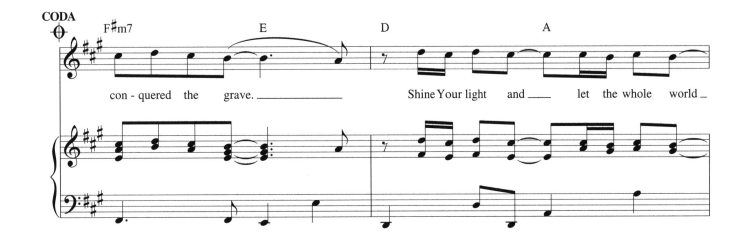

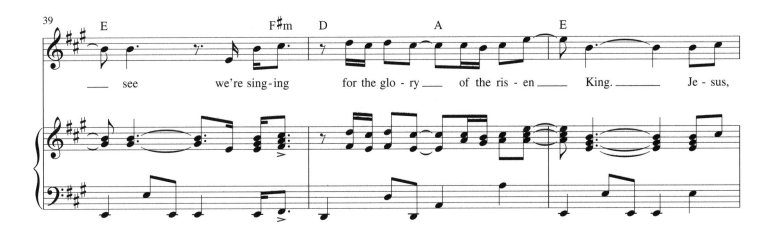

for the glo - ry ___ of the ris - en ___ King. _____ Sav - ior, He can move the

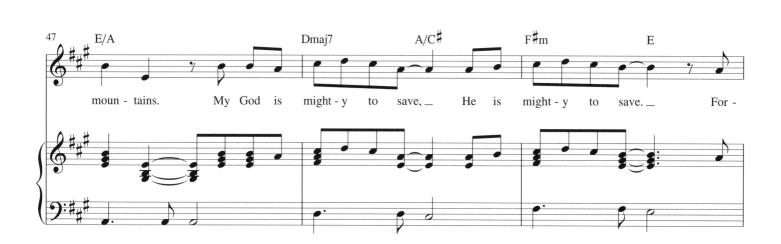

moun - tains. My God is might - y to save, __ He is might - y to save. __ For -

ev - er Au - thor of sal - va - tion, He rose and con-quered the grave, __ Je - sus

con - quered the grave. __ You're my Sav - ior, You can move the

moun - tains. God, You are might - y to save, _ You are might - y to save. _ For -

ev - er Au - thor of sal - va - tion, You rose and con - quered the grave, _ yes, You

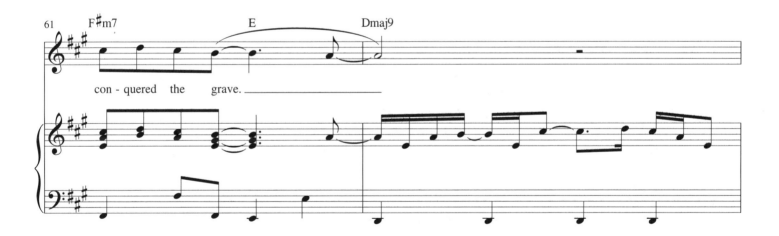

con - quered the grave. _____

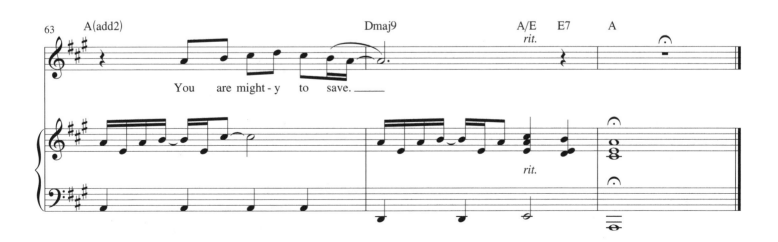

You are might - y to save. _____

Our God

Words and Music by JONAS MYRIN,
CHRIS TOMLIN, MATT REDMAN
and JESSE REEVES

Wa - ter You turned _ in - to wine, _

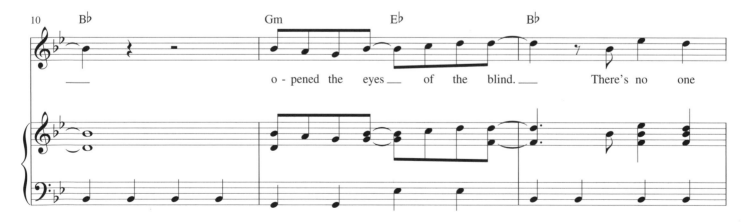

_ o - pened the eyes _ of the blind. _ There's no one

like You, ____ none like _____ You. _____

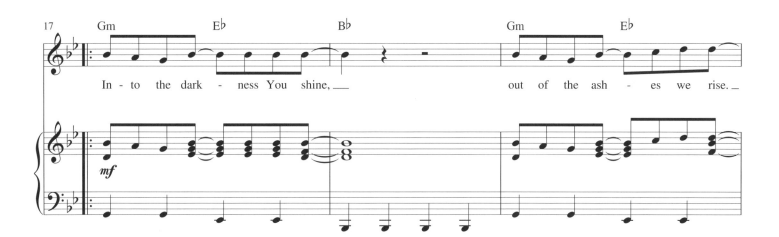

In - to the dark - ness You shine, ____ out of the ash - es we rise. ___

____ There's no one like You, ____ none like ____

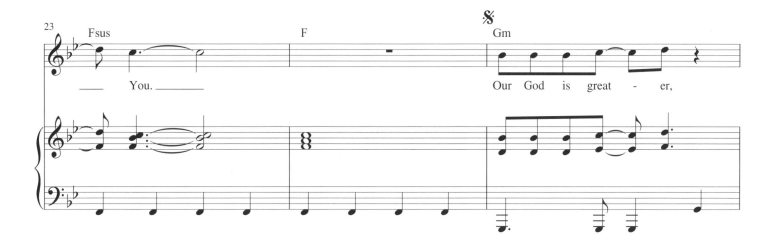

____ You. _____ Our God is great - er,

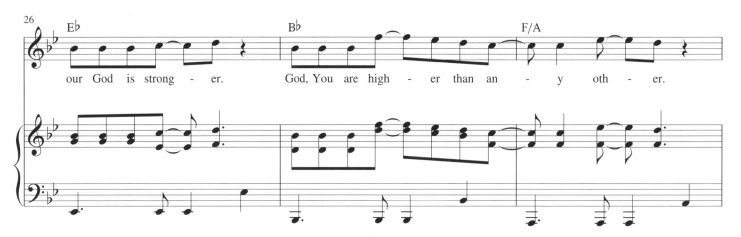

our God is strong - er. God, You are high - er than an - y oth - er.

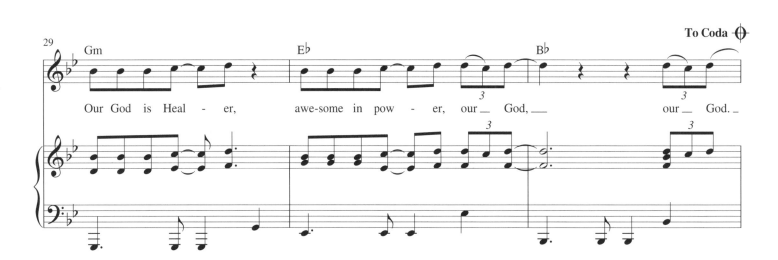

Our God is Heal - er, awe-some in pow - er, our God, our God.

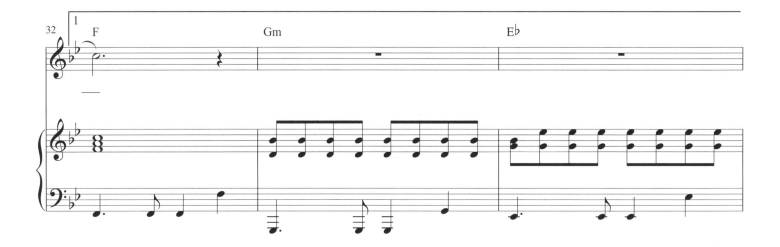

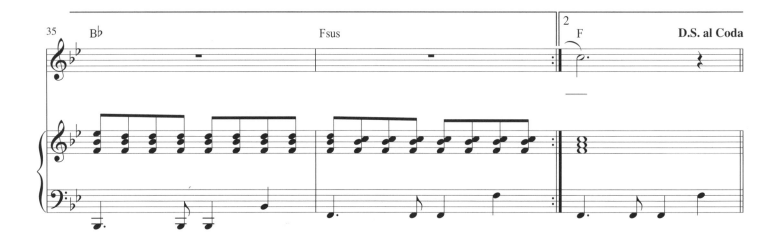

CODA

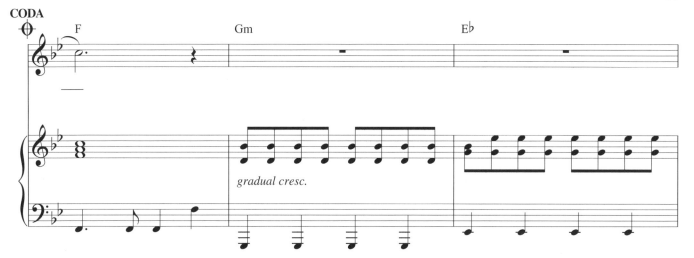

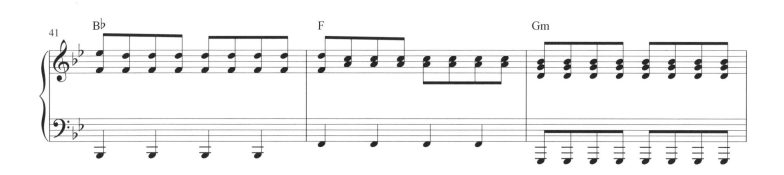

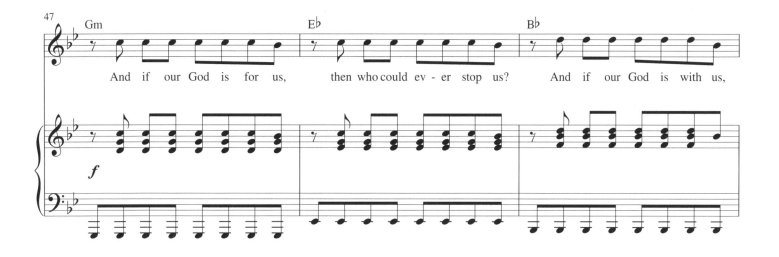

And if our God is for us, then who could ev - er stop us? And if our God is with us,

then what could stand a - gainst? _ And if our God is for us, then who could ev - er stop us?

And if our God is with us, then what could stand a - gainst? _

What could stand a - gainst? _

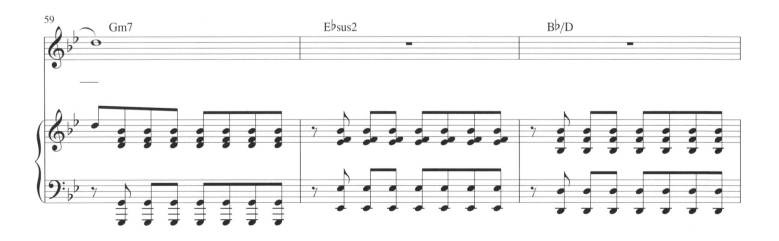

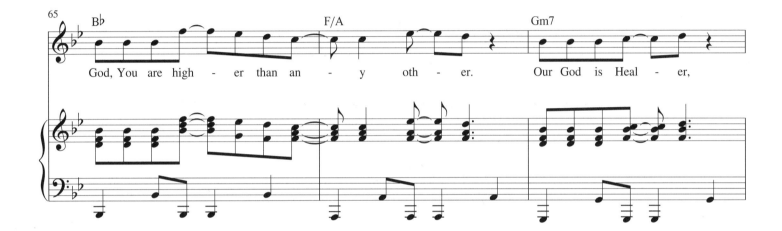

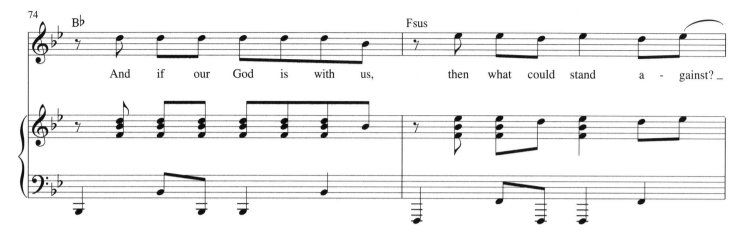

And if our God is with us, then what could stand a - gainst? _

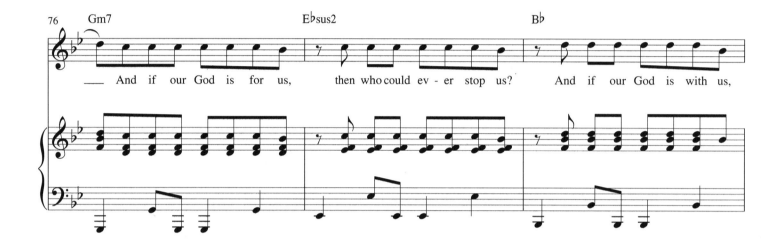

_ And if our God is for us, then who could ev - er stop us? And if our God is with us,

then what could stand a - gainst? _

Then what could stand a - gainst? ___

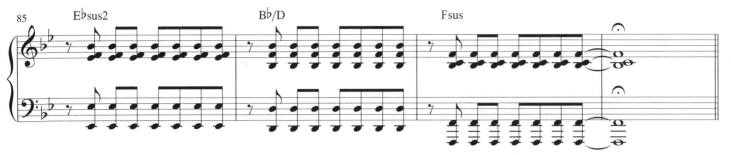

Our God is great - er, our God is strong - er. God, You are high - er than an -

- y oth - er. Our God is Heal - er, awe-some in pow - er, our __ God, __

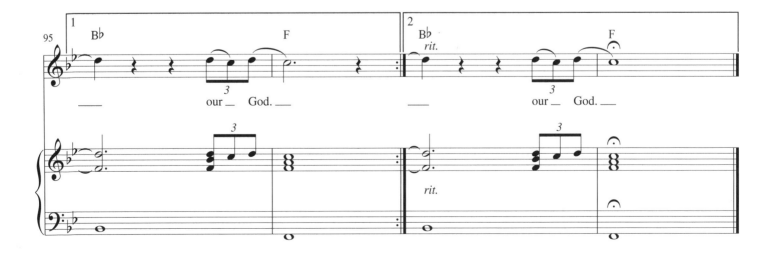

__ our __ God. __

our __ God. __

Revelation Song

Words and Music by
JENNIE LEE RIDDLE

Wor - thy is the Lamb who was slain. Ho - ly, ho - ly is He. ___

Sing a new song to ___ Him who sits on

Heav-en's mer - cy seat. ___ ___

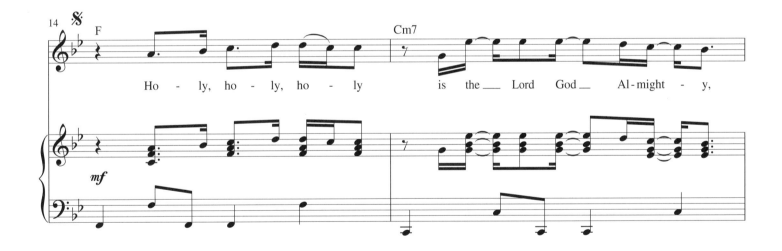

Ho - ly, ho - ly, ho - ly is the ___ Lord God ___ Al-might - y,

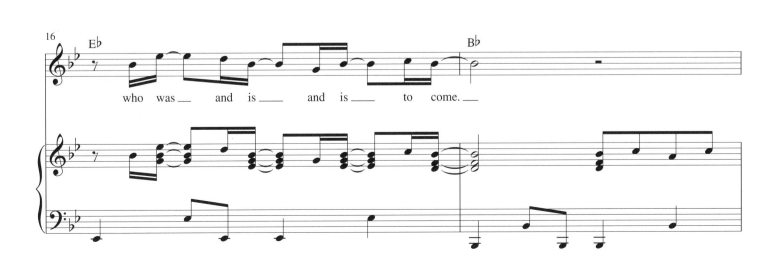

who was ___ and is ___ and is ___ to come. ___

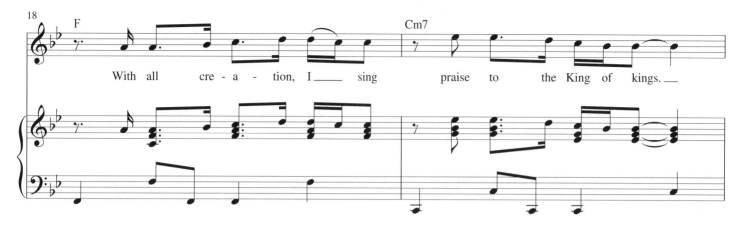

With all cre-a-tion, I___ sing praise to the King of kings.___

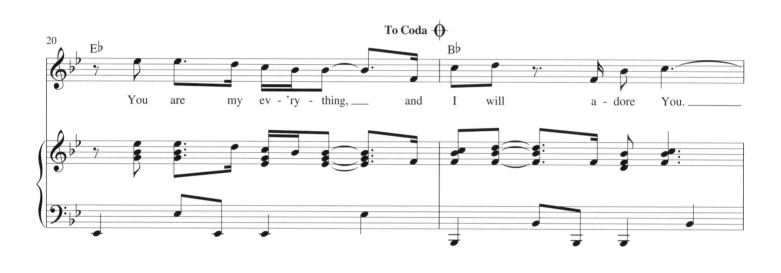

You are my ev-'ry-thing,___ and I will a-dore You.___

To Coda

Yeah,___ I will___ a-dore You.___

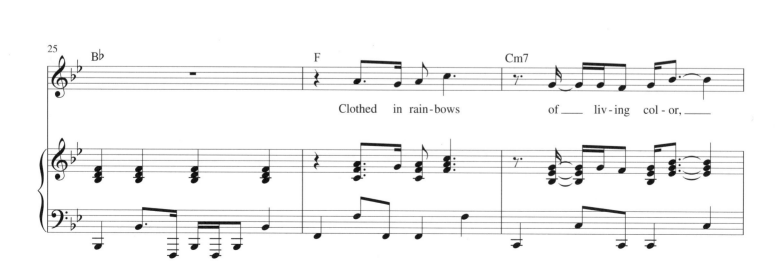

Clothed in rain-bows of ___ liv-ing col-or,___

flash - es of light - ning, rolls ____ of thun - der.

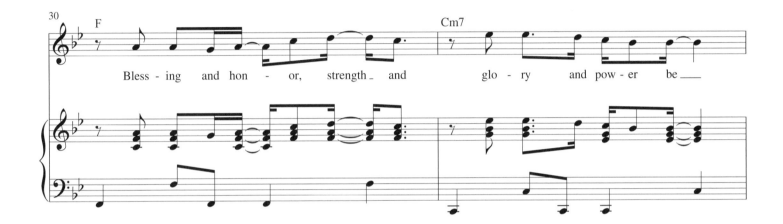

Bless - ing and hon - or, strength ___ and glo - ry and pow - er be ____

D.S. al Coda

to You, ____ the on - ly wise ____ King, yeah. ____

CODA

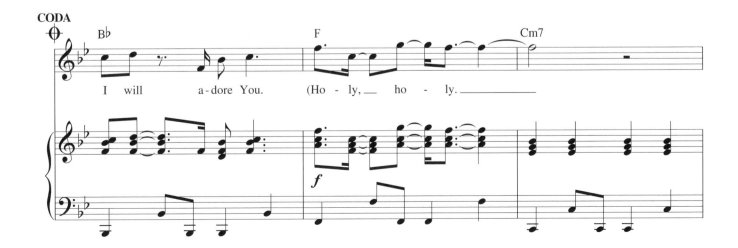

I will a - dore You. (Ho - ly, ____ ho - ly. ____

You are __ ho - ly.) _____ Filled with won - der,

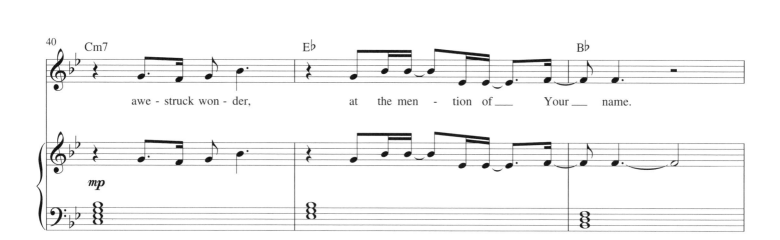

awe - struck won - der, at the men - tion of __ Your __ name.

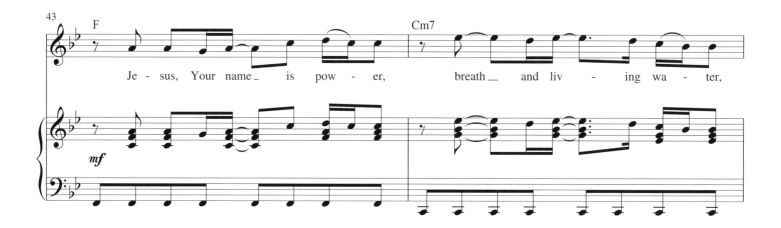

Je - sus, Your name __ is pow - er, breath __ and liv - ing wa - ter,

such __ a mar - v'lous mys - ter - y, _____ yeah. _____

Ho - ly, ho - ly, ho - ly is the __ Lord God __ Al-might - y,

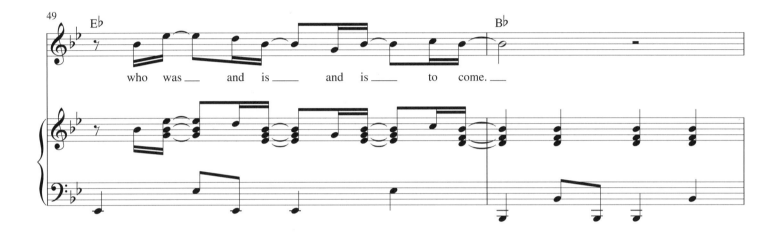

who was __ and is __ and is __ to come. __

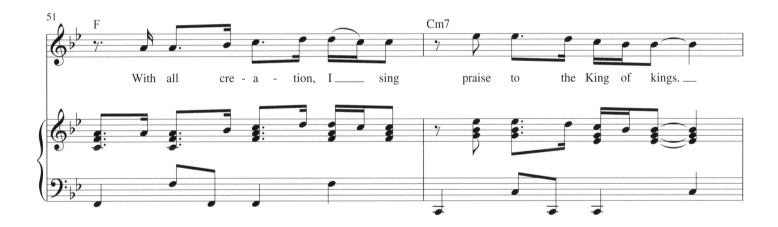

With all cre - a - tion, I __ sing praise to the King of kings. __

You are my ev - 'ry - thing, __ and I will a - dore You.

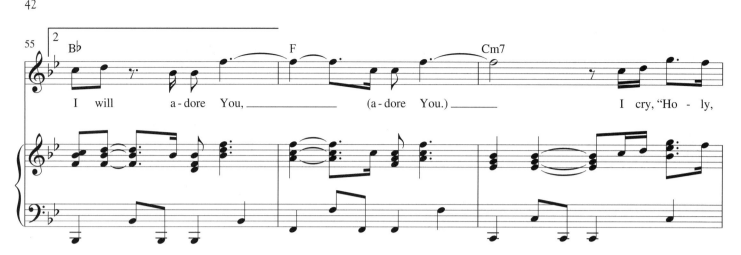

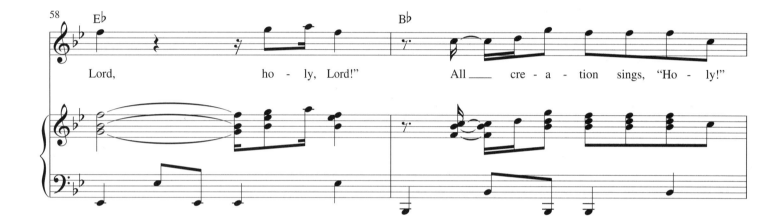

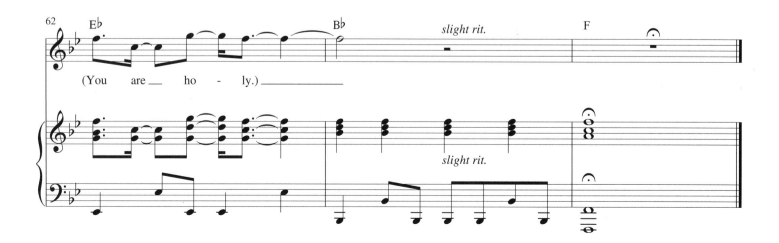

Stronger

Words and Music by BEN FIELDING
and REUBEN MORGAN

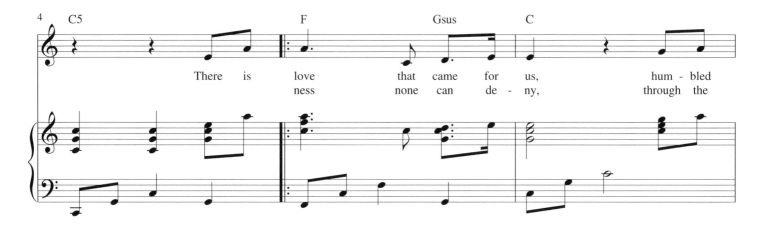

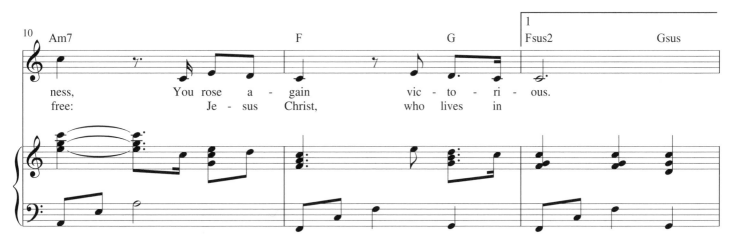

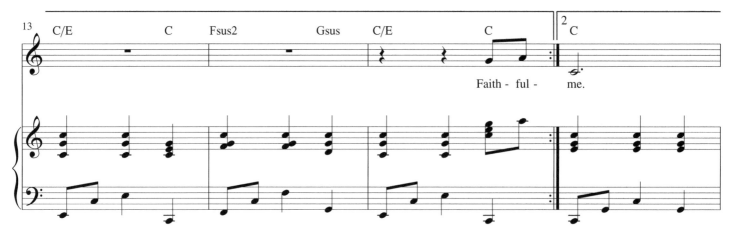

Faith - ful - me.

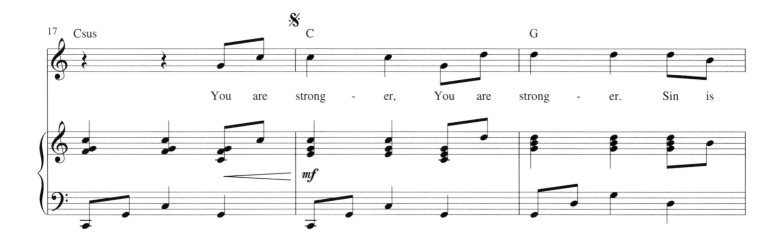

You are strong - er, You are strong - er. Sin is

bro - ken, You have saved me. It is writ - ten: Christ is

To Coda ⊕

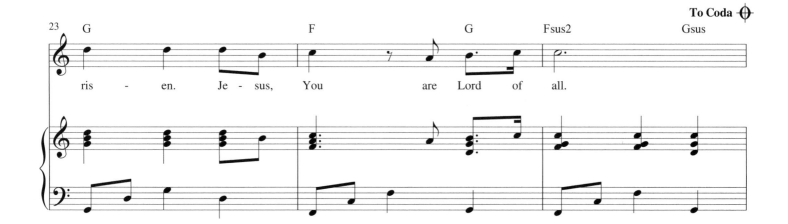

ris - en. Je - sus, You are Lord of all.

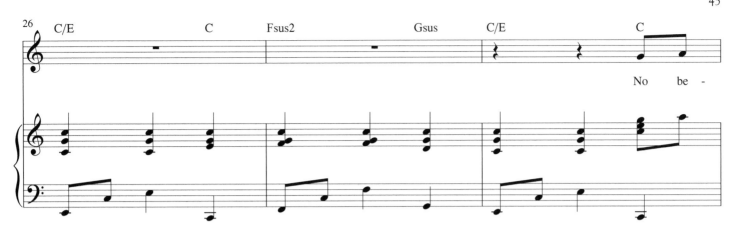

No be -

gin - ning and no end, You're my hope and my de -

fense. You came to seek and save the lost. You paid it

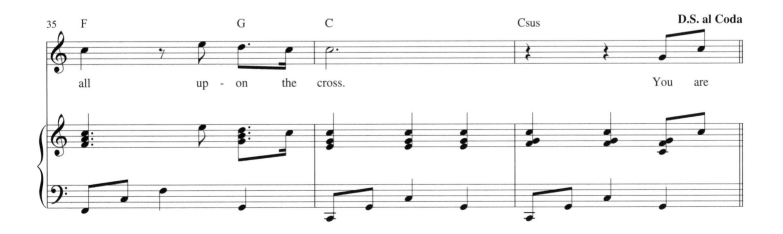

all up - on the cross. You are

D.S. al Coda

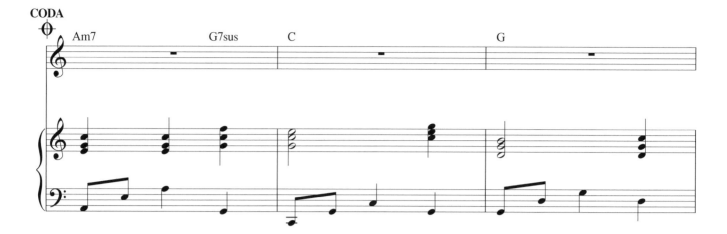

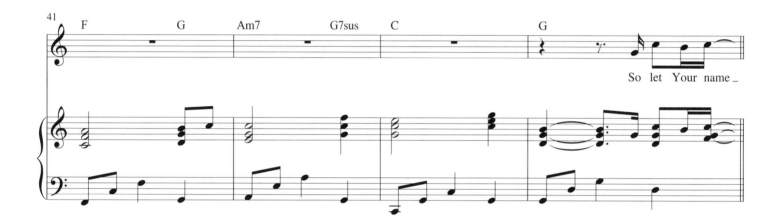

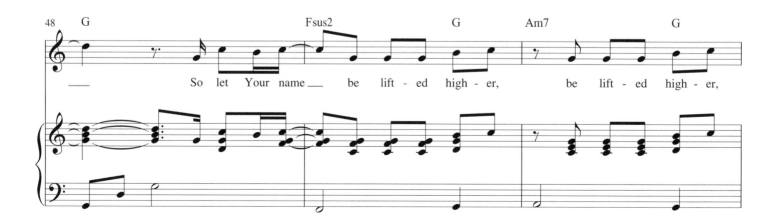

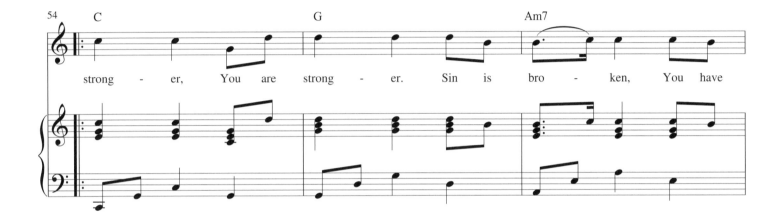

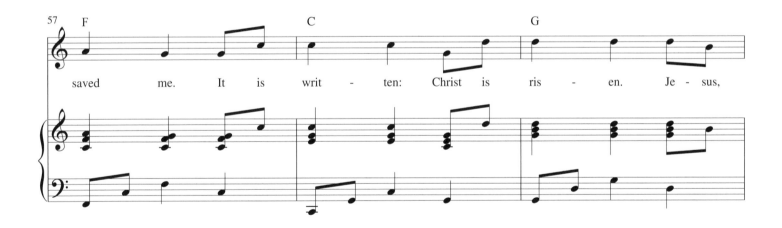

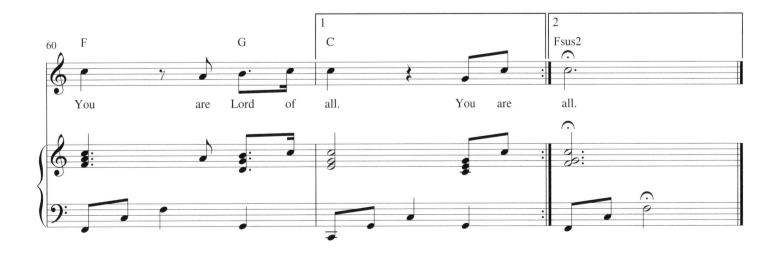

Your Name

Words and Music by PAUL BALOCHE
and GLENN PACKIAM

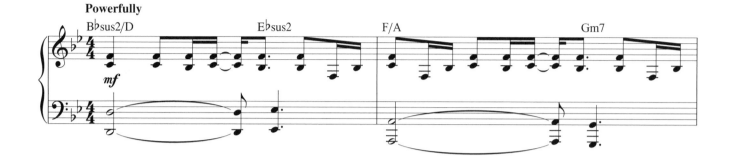

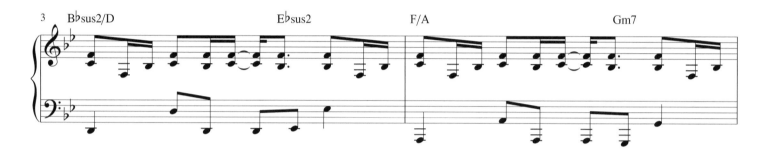

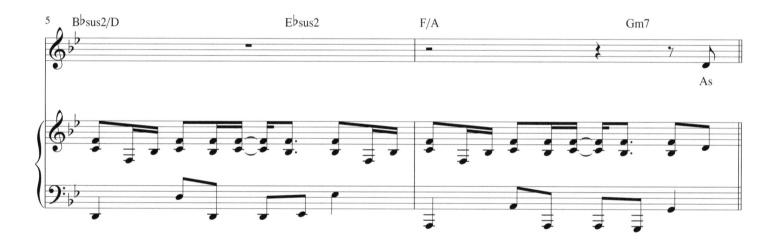

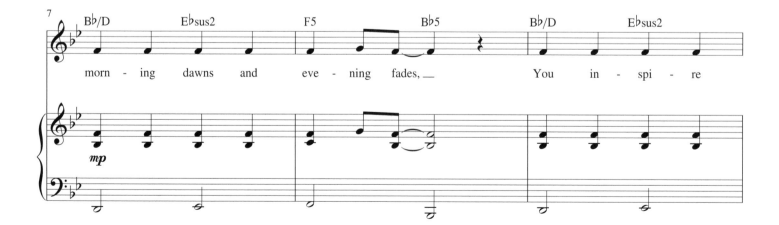

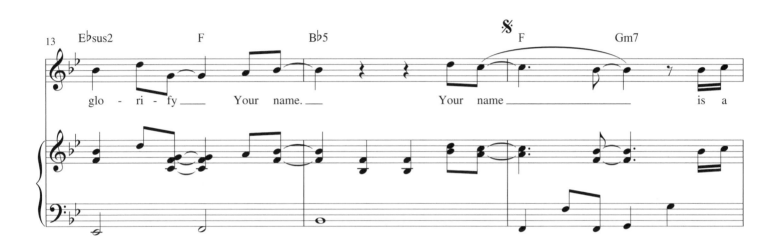

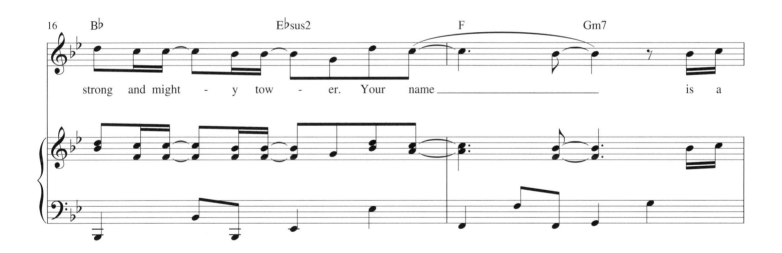

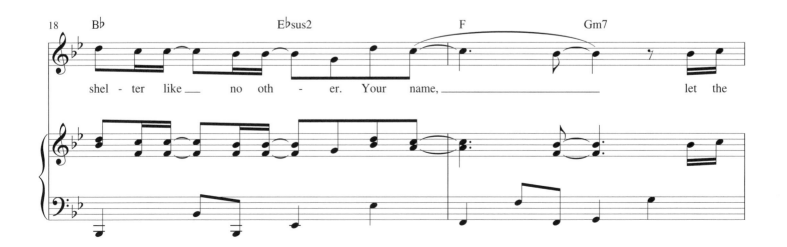

To Coda ⊕

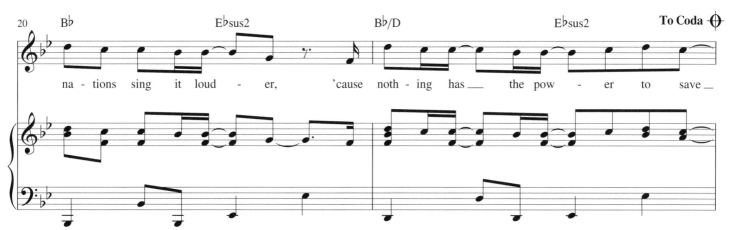

na - tions sing it loud - er, 'cause noth - ing has __ the pow - er to save __

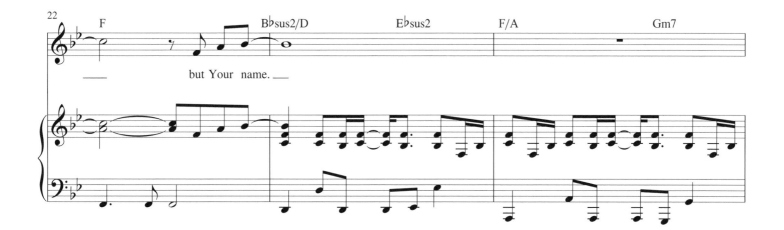

__ but Your name. __

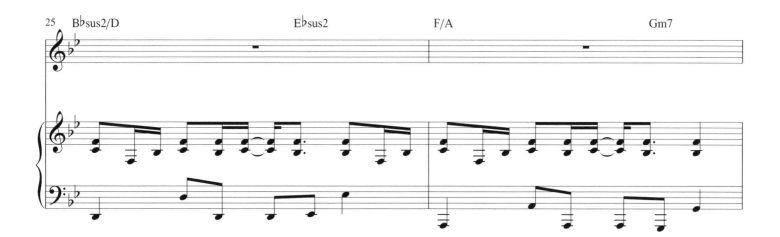

Je - sus, in Your name we pray, __ come and fill our __

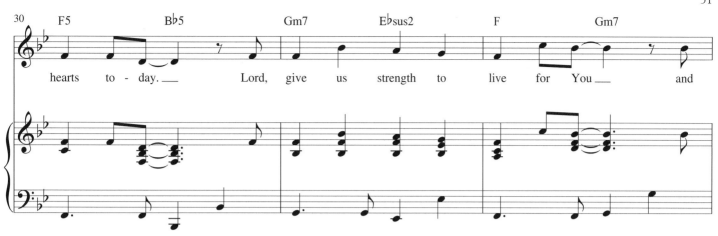

hearts to - day. ___ Lord, give us strength to live for You ___ and

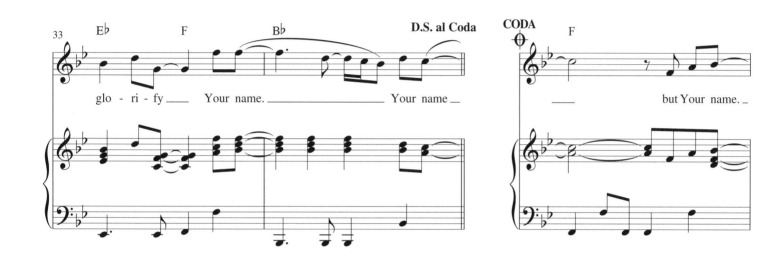

glo - ri - fy ___ Your name. ___ Your name ___

D.S. al Coda

CODA

but Your name. ___

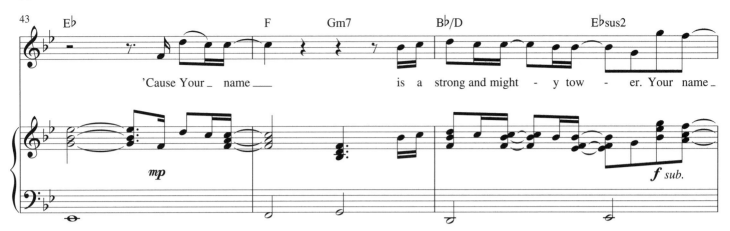

'Cause Your name _____ is a strong and might - y tow - er. Your name _____

_____ is a shel - ter like _ no oth - er. Your name, _____

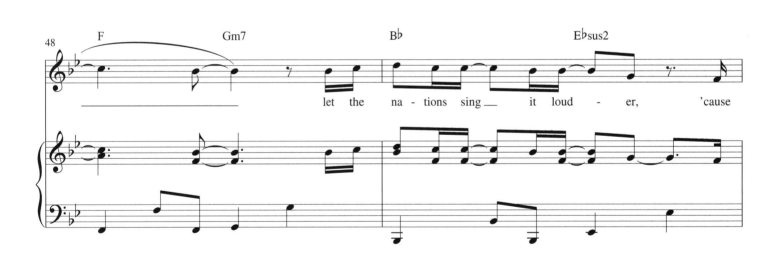

let the na - tions sing _ it loud - er, 'cause

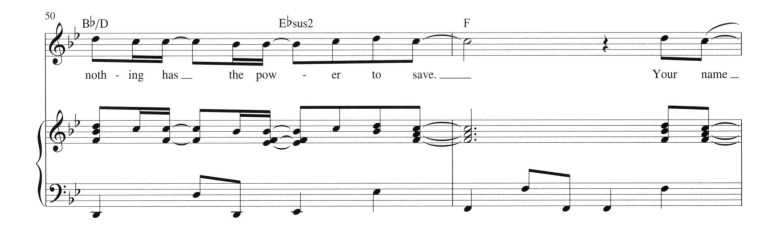

noth - ing has _ the pow - er to save. _____ Your name _____

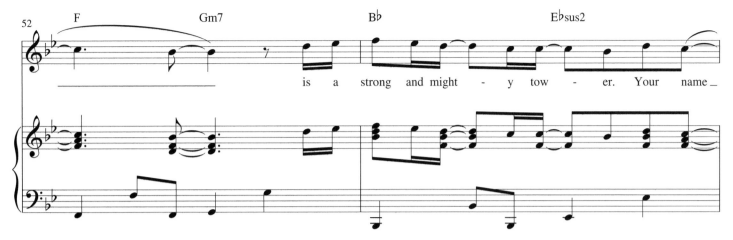

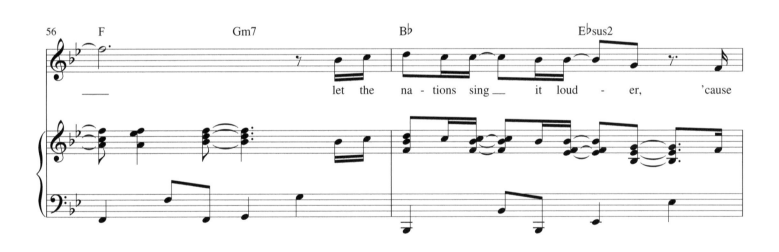

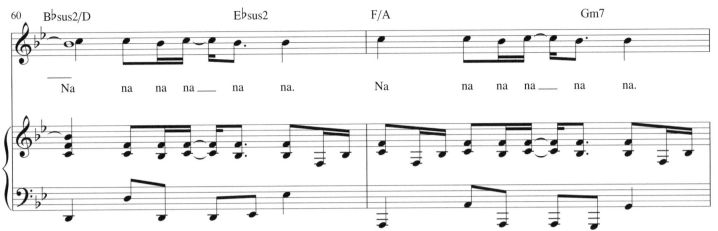

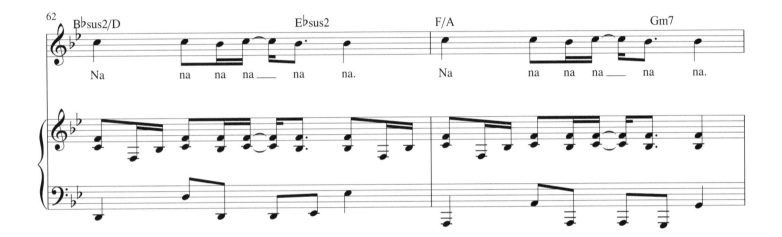

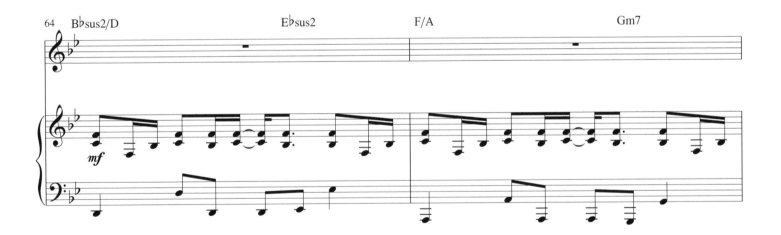

Whom Shall I Fear
(God of Angel Armies)

Words and Music by CHRIS TOMLIN,
ED CASH and SCOTT CASH

You crush the en-e-my un-der-neath my feet. You are my sword and shield,

though trou-bles lin-ger still. _____ Whom shall _ I _____ fear?

I know who goes be-fore me, I know who stands be-hind.

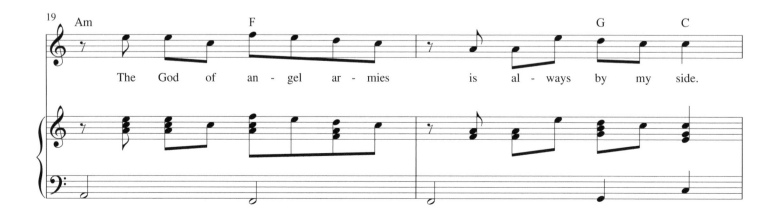

The God of an-gel ar-mies is al-ways by my side.

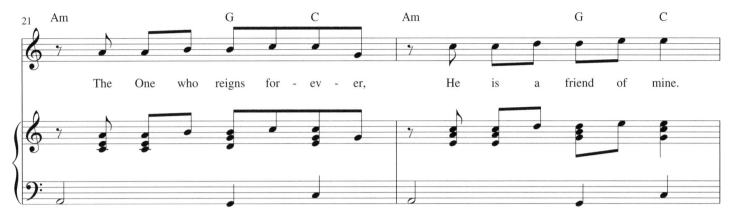

The One who reigns for-ev-er, He is a friend of mine.

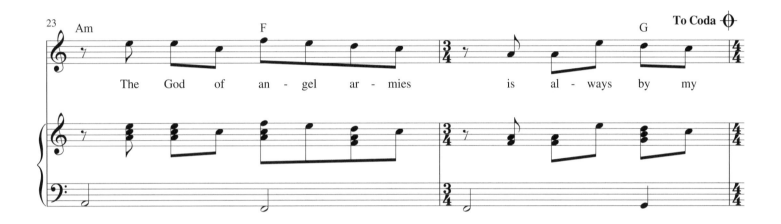

The God of an-gel ar-mies is al-ways by my

side.

My strength is in Your name, for You a-lone can save. You will de-liv-er me;

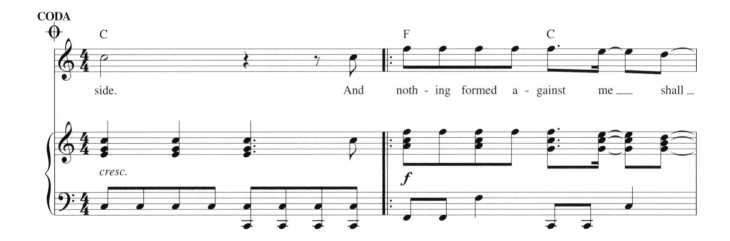

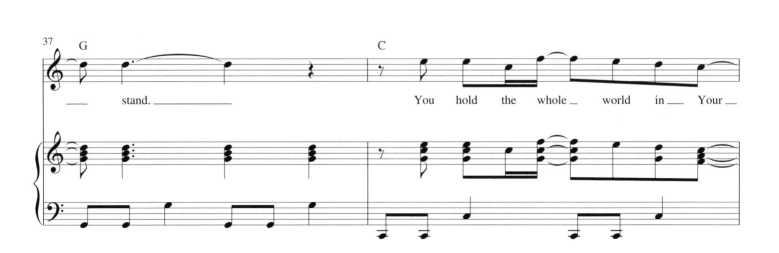

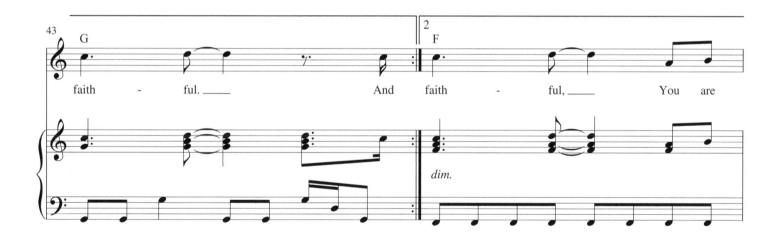

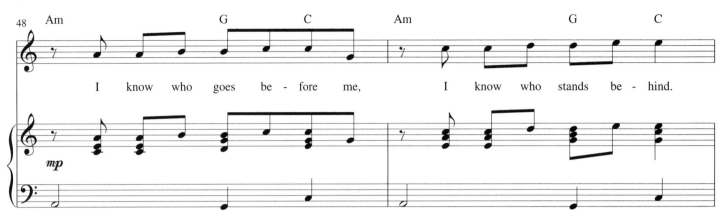

I know who goes be - fore me, I know who stands be - hind.

The God of an - gel ar - mies is al - ways by my side.

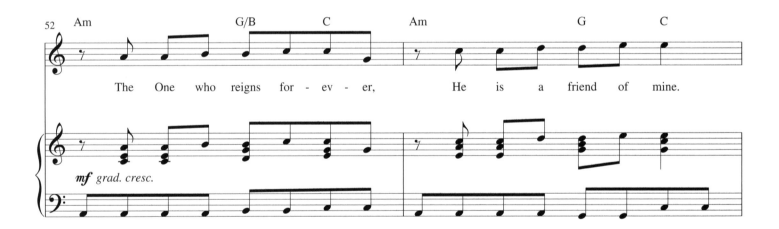

The One who reigns for - ev - er, He is a friend of mine.

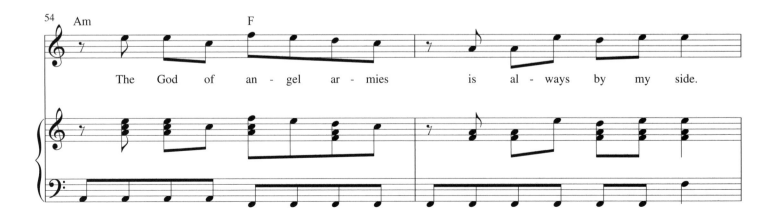

The God of an - gel ar - mies is al - ways by my side.

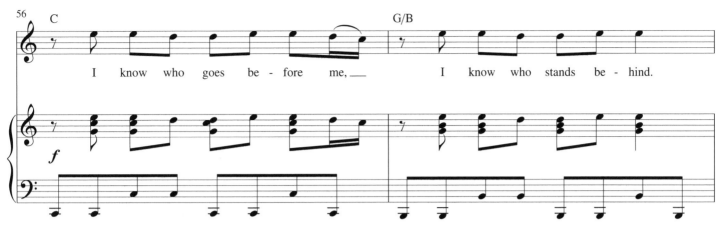

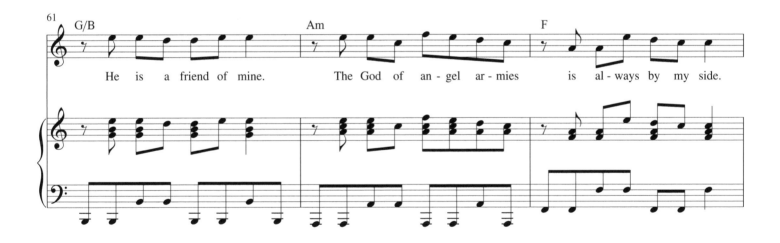

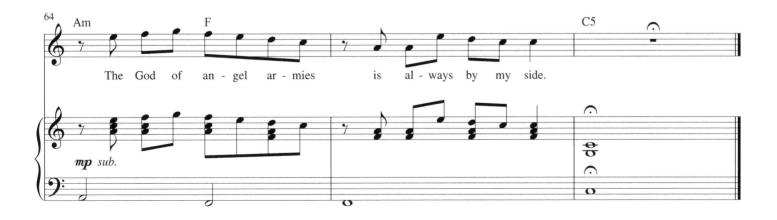

Your Grace is Enough

Words and Music by
MATT MAHER

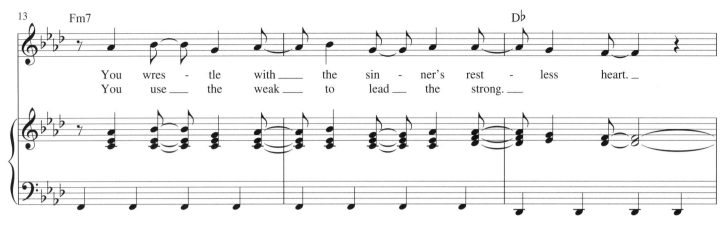

You wres - tle with ___ the sin - ner's rest - less heart. ___
You use ___ the weak ___ to lead ___ the strong. ___

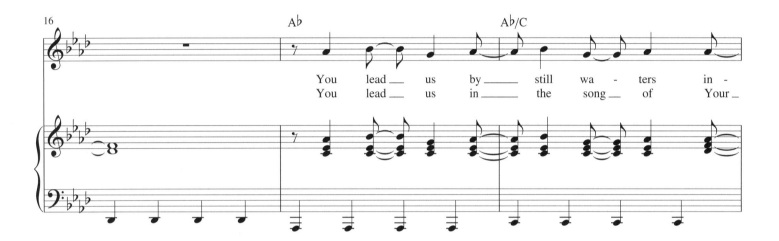

You lead ___ us by ___ still wa - ters in -
You lead ___ us in ___ the song ___ of Your

___ to mer - cy, and noth - ing can ___
___ sal - va - tion, and all ___ Your peo -

___ keep us ___ a - part. So re - mem - ber ___ Your
- ple sing ___ a - long. ___

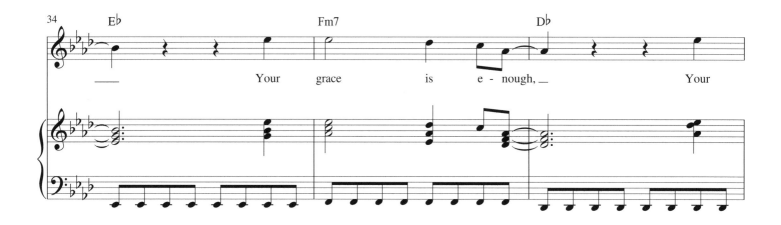

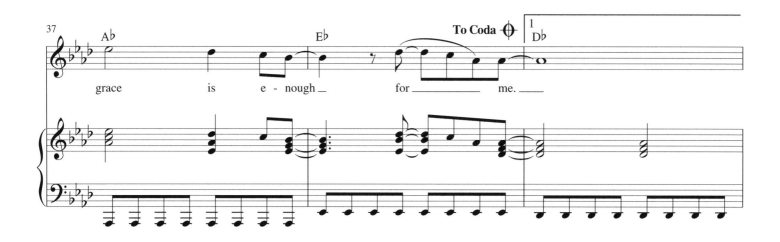

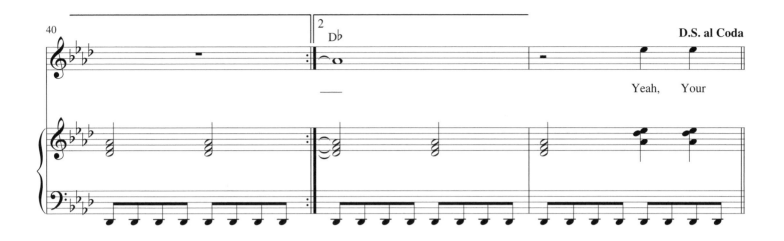

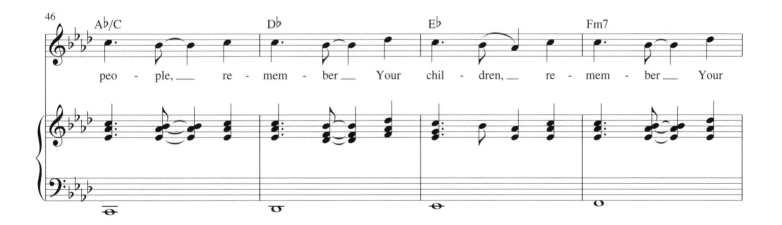

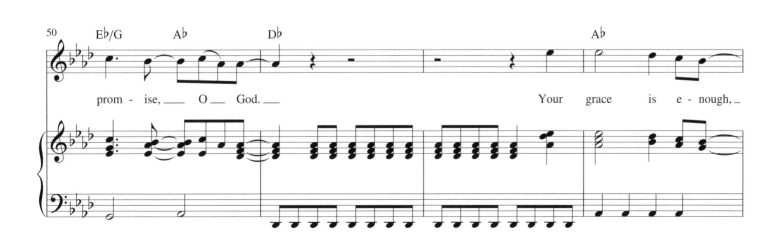

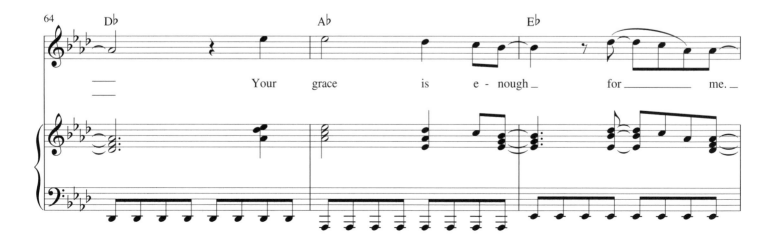

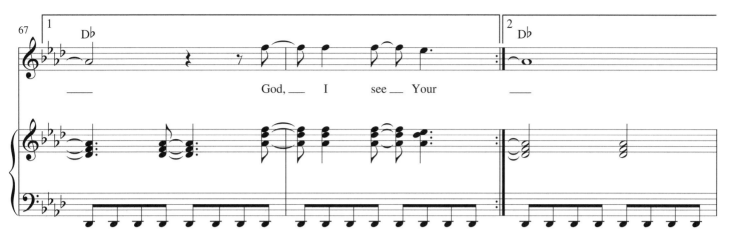

God, — I see — Your

For _____ me. _____

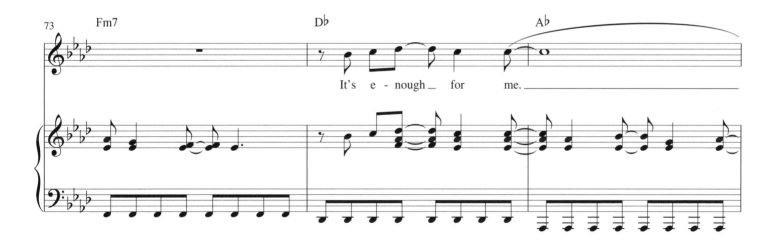

It's e - nough ___ for ___ me. _____

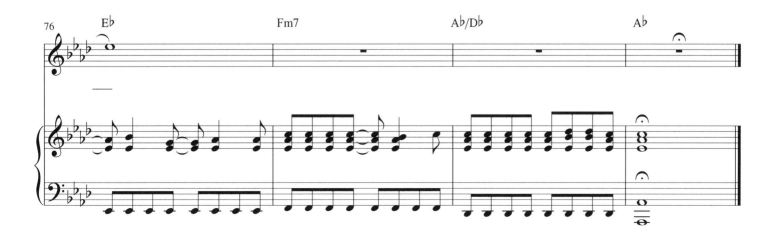